Creating

IN THE DIGITAL WORLD

By
Megan Kopp

YOUR
POSITIVE
Digital
Footprint

Author: Megan Kopp

Series research and development: Reagan Miller

Editors: Janine Deschenes, Reagan Miller,

Proofreader and indexer: Angela Kaelberer

Design, photo research, and prepress:
Margaret Amy Salter

Print coordinator: Katherine Berti

Photo Credits

iStock: front cover, kate_sept2004

Shutterstock: p 16, Tamisclao; p 17, omihay; p 19 (top left), oland; p 19 (top right), Ekaterina_Minaeva; p 29 (top), pianodiaphragm; p 29 (bottom), Peter Kotoff

All other images from Shutterstock

Library and Archives Canada Cataloguing in Publication

Kopp, Megan, author
        Creating in the digital world / Megan Kopp.

(Your positive digital footprint)
Includes index.
Issued in print and electronic formats.
ISBN 978-0-7787-4601-0 (hardcover).--
ISBN 978-0-7787-4605-8 (softcover).--
ISBN 978-1-4271-2045-8 (HTML)

        1. Technology and the arts--Juvenile literature. 2. Art and technology--Juvenile literature. 3. Creative ability--Juvenile literature. 4. Digital media--Juvenile literature. I. Title.

NX180.T4K67 2018   j700.1'05   C2018-901259-5
                                                                    C2018-901260-9

Library of Congress Cataloging-in-Publication Data

CIP available at the Library of Congress

Crabtree Publishing Company

www.crabtreebooks.com   1-800-387-7650

Printed in the U.S.A./052018/BG20180327

Published in Canada
Crabtree Publishing
616 Welland Ave.
St. Catharines, Ontario
L2M 5V6

Published in the United States
Crabtree Publishing
PMB 59051
350 Fifth Avenue, 59th Floor
New York, New York 10118

Published in the United Kingdom
Crabtree Publishing
Maritime House
Basin Road North, Hove
BN41 1WR

Published in Australia
Crabtree Publishing
3 Charles Street
Coburg North
VIC, 3058

Contents

A World of Opportunity

How do you express yourself? When you have a story to tell or an idea to share, do you grab a paper and pen—or reach for your phone, camera, or laptop? In the not-so-far-away past, people had few options with which they could express themselves. Today, **digital** tools can create such things as vlogs, audio **mashups**, interactive presentations, and amazing art. Using digital tools opens up a world of opportunity with creativity!

Using digital tools and your creative mind, you can create amazing things—from digital scrapbooks to art that comes to life!

Digital citizenship means that you contribute positively to the digital community in a safe and meaningful way.

When you use digital technology, you are a digital citizen. This opens up a world of opportunity. But there are also responsibilities and costs that come with digital citizenship. Every time you make a comment, send a message, post a photo, visit a website, use a **search engine**, or sign up for an **app**, you leave a digital trail online called your **digital footprint**. Part of being a good digital citizen means that you are safe in your online practices. But it also means much more.

Digital citizenship also means that you can be empowered to use tools and contribute your ideas and creativity to a **digital community**. This book gives you advice on how to choose the right platforms and tools to reach your creative goal. It guides you in how to use feedback to improve and grow as a digital creator. It also offers the knowledge you need to make sure that you get credit for your work and when to give credit to others.

Consumer to Creator

From watching videos and listening to music to reading **social media** posts, you might spend a lot of screen time consuming, or taking in, digital content. Active or **productive** digital citizens aim to balance their online activities between consuming and creating content. They look for ways to use technology to solve problems, help others, and contribute their ideas to the digital world. They also use creativity to find ways to make a positive impact on others. In recent years, new digital tools have made it possible for people to create and share digital content. These tools provide opportunities to write, record, design, build, and **code**.

A 2015 study by Common Sense Media found that tweens mainly use digital devices to consume content. Only 3% of their activities involved creating content, such as making art, composing music, or coding. How does your screen time compare? Imagine what you could do if you take a little slice of time spent consuming content and put it towards creating something.

Becoming a digital citizen is a lifelong process. Our digital world is in constant motion. Changes happen fast. New tools come and old ones are left behind. We need to keep learning, creating, and moving forward in the digital world. As lifetime digital citizens, we need to keep sharing our creations, especially those that may benefit others.

How can you use your interests, talents, and skills to create digital content?

What is Digital Creation?

What does digital creation look like? Anything you make online with digital tools is digital creation. Digital creation gives us the opportunity share our skills and interests. Do you like LEGOs, skateboarding, hockey, hip-hop music, or drawing? No matter what you like, there are digital projects you can create to share your passion.

You can start a blog or contribute to one already created. Record a **podcast** to share your ideas on any topic you wish. Design an **infographic** that displays your knowledge in a visual way. Create a website, design a digital poster, produce a YouTube video, plan a social media campaign to draw attention to an issue, build an interactive timeline, develop an app, or even learn to write code.

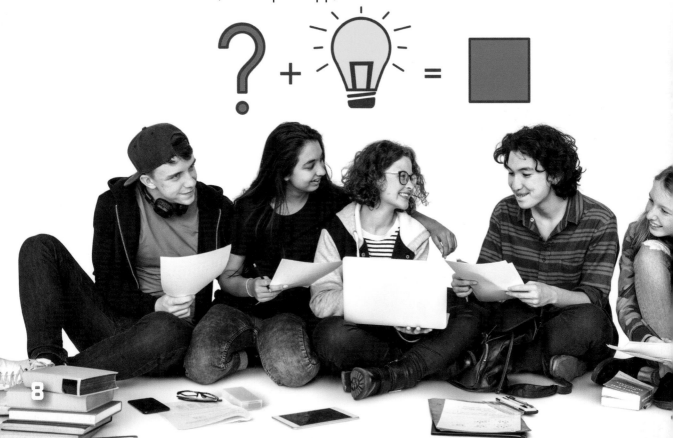

Coding helps you break down problems and teaches you how to solve them. When you code, you develop skills, such as perseverance and grit, that will continue to help you in the future.

There are many different coding programs that allow you to create different things. One program, Scratch (https://scratch.mit.edu), makes it easy to create interactive stories, games, music, or art. Scratch teaches math, programming, and creative expression through technology. While learning to code, kids create animations, games, and models.

DIGITAL DYNAMO

DIGITAL DYNAMO: REBECCA GARCIA, CODER

CODERDOJONYC

For Rebecca Garcia, technology is fun. It is a tool for creating and for building. Rebecca cofounded CoderdojoNYC to create resources that make technology accessible for different people. Coderdojo offers free clubs that teach young people around the world coding languages. She was named a U.S. White House Champion of Change for "Tech Inclusion." She is an active digital citizen because she shares her knowledge with others.

Starting from Scratch

We live in a world where information is at our fingertips. It is easy to access, copy, and share. You probably already know that when you use another person's images, words, or videos, you need to give them **credit** (read more about this on page 12). But how is your own creative work protected? When you create and publish a journal, sketch an original cartoon, or make a skateboarding video, how do you protect it from people that might want to borrow parts of it? How do you stop them from taking the whole thing and calling it their own?

The answer is **copyright**. You might have seen "Copyright" or "©" on credits pages in books, at the bottom of website pages, or in YouTube videos. Copyright means that the person or organization that created the work gets to decide how it is used.

As the creator, you have control over how your work can be used by others. You have the final say on who is allowed to copy, adapt or change, **distribute**, display, or perform it. It is a good idea to put "Copyright" or the symbol © and the year at the end of your work, but it is not necessary. All original work is automatically copyrighted.

Creative works are copyrighted, but ideas are not. If you share an idea about a one-of-a-kind comic-book character with someone else, they can draw it— and the drawing is their own. But if you shared a picture that you drew of the character, it is copyrighted. You created the image of the character, so it is yours and only yours to use or to give people permission to use.

The Wonderful Wizard of Oz, written by L. Frank Baum in 1900, is in the public domain. People can use it to create something new, such as this image.

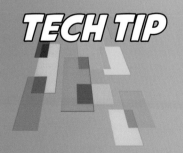

TECH TIP

Public Domain

Copyright does not last forever. Today, it lasts only for 70 years after the creator dies. The work then goes into the public domain. The public domain is works that are not protected by copyright and are free to use. Anyone can sell, change, or adapt work in the public domain. In the United States, any work created before 1923 is automatically in the public domain. As well, work done by U.S. government employees is free to use. Check out the Library of Congress (loc.gov) for a collection of resources in the public domain.

Fair is Fair

You have just finished a Google image search and found the perfect picture to add to your blog. Plunk it in and you are done. Or are you? What are your responsibilities when using the work of others, and what rights do you have as a creator? Do you know who owns the copyright? Did you credit the creator? Just because it is on the Internet does not mean it is free to use.

Respect is a two-way street. If you want other people to respect the copyright of your work, you need to respect their rights as well. If you copy someone else's work and call it your own, it is called plagiarism. You have stolen someone else's work. Luckily, there are ways to use people's work fairly by giving them credit.

When you quote your favorite author in a book report or look up ideas to quote in a vlog, you need to credit the copyright owner.

Fair use laws allow you to use other people's work in certain situations. According to these laws, you can copy small amounts of copyrighted works for education and research. If the amount is small, you are not selling the work, and your use of the work does not affect the owner's opportunity to **profit** from their work, then it is usually considered fair use. For example, if short quotations from different sources are used to create a new message about a topic, that is fair use. But remember, even with snippets of work, it is always important to credit the copyright owner.

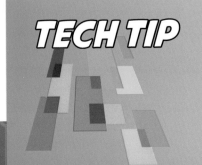

TECH TIP

If you want to use 20 seconds of a Justin Bieber song to start a video for a school project that will only be shared with your classmates, it is fair use. If you download the entire song and put it in a video which is going up on a YouTube channel for the world to see, that is not fair use.

13

Creative Commons

Creators of many kinds of work have come together to share and collaborate in our global digital community. Creative Commons is an organization that has come up with an easier way to legally share, use, and reuse material. More than half a billion creative works can be found here. They include such things as photos, books, paintings, song lyrics, podcasts, and video. Creators give permission for their works to be shared on Creative Commons. There are different **licenses**, or agreements, on how works in the Creative Commons can be used.

Do you have an eye for photography? You can choose to share your photos on Creative Commons for another digital citizen to view and use.

Creative Commons has six different types of agreements. The most open one is called Creative Commons **Attribution**. It is often written as CC BY. This license allows you to take a piece of work and do whatever you want with it. You can share it, add text, cro it, draw on it, and even sell it.

Other Creative Commons licenses limit the types of changes that can be made and do not allow images to be sold. The Creative Commons Attribution - NoDerivatives (CC BY-ND) allows people to use the image or other work, but they cannot change it in any way. It must be used exactly as it appears.

To find images, audio recordings, videos or text, you can go the Creative Commons search page at http://search.creativecommons.org.

Use the Commons search to find what you are looking for. Be sure you understand the license and what you can or cannot do with the work. Don't forget to add attribution either below the work or on a special attribution page at the end of your creation.

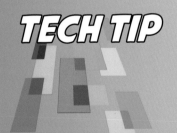

How to give an attribution

- Open the Creative Commons and click on "search the commons."
- Select the Google images box.
- Type "what do you want to create today" in the search query box.
- Click on the first image. Under the date, you should see a small black circle around a black figure. To the right it says "some rights reserved." Click on this for the CC license.
- Every attribution should include TASL (Title, Author, Source, License).
- The best attribution for this image would be: "What Do You Want to Create Today" (linked to source) by Wesley Fryer (linked to author's profile page) is licensed under CC BY 2.0 (linked to license deed)

Movie Over Spielberg

Reminders

iMovie

What do *Jurassic Park*, *Transformers*, and *Men in Black* all have in common? Each was a series of multiple films produced by Steven Spielberg—costing millions of dollars each to produce. While you may not be in the same league as Spielberg yet, digital movie creation is becoming simpler every day.

Like any Hollywood production, digital creations start with questions. What would I like to create? What are the best tools for this project? Do I have the skills necessary to use these tools correctly? If not, where can I go to learn more? Who can I ask for help?

Apple's iMovie for iPad makes it easy to repurpose work that has been done by others. The program comes loaded with iMovie trailers, or short pieces of film. You can pick one of these trailers, add images, text, or photos and create a short movie.

Minecraft's creative mode allows your imagination to fly! To play Minecraft, you will need to buy the game, download it, and install it on your computer.

Beyond movies, there are countless apps and programs that let your creativity shine. Do you want to write a book? Book Creator for iPad is an easy-to-use tool for creating and publishing digital books available for purchase from the App Store. Want to show off knowledge about your favorite sport? Create a slideshow by editing photos of your skiing tricks and uploading them to Buncee (www.edu.buncee.com). If you don't have your own photos, the website has an image library that includes graphics and photos to help you make a presentation about the sport. Love video games? Use Minecraft (www.minecraft.net) to create totally new and original environments in creative mode.

TECH TOOLBOX

StoryboardThat (www.storyboardthat.com) is a free tool for creating cool comics and storyboards. Pick a scene, add some customizable characters and text, and in no time at all you have a comic waiting to be shared with friends and family.

Creating a Mashup

A mashup is a name that describes something new created by combining many different existing sources. You might immediately think of catchy song mashups. But mashups can be used in a lot of different ways! They are a fantastic way for many digital citizens to collaborate. For example, you could add photos of skateboard parks onto a Google map. There are many tools to help you with a digital mashup.

Song mashups layer sounds and lyrics from one song over another.

Hear Me was a mashup of many creative works made by youth. It was developed by the CREATE Lab at Carnegie Mellon University, and raised awareness about issues faced by young people. Hear Me was a tool built for kids to tell their stories in different ways and be heard by other digital citizens. Using writing, art, audio, video, or digital storytelling, kids used their stories to inspire social change. Although the project was deactivated in December of 2017, you can still listen to the stories and podcasts and read the blog for creative inspiration at http://www.hear-me.net.

Toontastic 3D (https://toontastic.withgoogle.com) is a creative storytelling app that lets you draw, animate, narrate, and record your own cartoon on a tablet or phone. GarageBand is a music creation app for Mac computers. It helps you compose original tunes or mashup previously published tunes.

A word cloud is a type of mashup. Wordle (www.wordle.net) is a fun tool to create word clouds. It is a creative way to organize and display a set of words about a topic. Try it out with your friends! Ask them who their favorite recording artist is and write down their answers. There may be multiples of the same answer. That's okay. When these words are put into the program, the words that appear most often will be larger than others.

Failing Forward

Do you think that the first person to write code for your favorite game just got up one day and knew how to do it? Do you think every digital artist was born with the skills they need to create a masterpiece? No and no. Failure is part of the creative process. It is part of learning. The important point is not to fear failure. Do not ever let it stop you from learning and moving forward.

Every creative project starts with an idea. Because there are so many digital tools available to help you get creative, you need to ask yourself some questions:

- Which tool is the best one for the job? Why?
- Do I have the skills I need to be able to use this tool?
- Is there another option?

By asking youself these questions, you are thinking **critically**. Critical thinking is all about asking questions, moving forward, and analyzing the results. If the first option doesn't work, move on to the next. Question, try, analyze and keep going until you find the tool that works.

ry creative person has to make choice to accept that failure is t of the learning process. They ose to see failure as a step ng the way to success. Failure ust feedback. When things do t work, ask yourself why. Think out how you could fix the oblem or do things differently e next time. It is all about signing, testing, and improving.

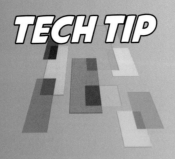

In 1985, Steve Jobs was let go from Apple, the very company he started in his garage. Have you ever heard of Apple's Lisa computer? It never sold well. In fact, it was generally considered a failure. Sales were crashing. Nothing new was being invented. The competition was taking over. Twelve years later, Apple was nearly bankrupt. Steve Jobs came back. He focused on creating new products. From iPod to iPad to iPhone, success came after failure. Today, Apple is the most valuable brand in the world.

DIGITAL DYNAMO

NATE BUTKUS: FEARLESS PODCASTER

Nate Butkus loves science. He loves it so much that at age five he asked his dad, Eric, to help him start a podcast. The idea of failure never entered Nate's young mind when he came up with his idea: "The Show About Science." While Eric is the tech behind the podcast, Nate is the creative genius with a passion for everything science. Nate is constantly learning, growing, and evolving as a podcast host. Nate's podcast can be found online at: https://soundcloud.com/the-show-about-science.

Smart and Secure

Being creative online is good, but it's important to make sure you are always being safe and secure when you share information and connect with others. These tips can help you make sure that you stay safe as a digital citizen.

- Never give away personal information. If you are signing up for a program with the permission of your parents or through your classroom, do not create a username that has your full name (first and last name).

- Choose strong passwords that are memorable, but don't use personal information such as your birthday. Don't share your password with anyone but your parents. Create different versions of the password for different accounts.

LOGIN
Password
ONLINE SECURITY
100%
PROTECTION
DATA
search?
Card ***

Remember that the Internet should be a positive place. Think of what you would like your digital footprint to look like. This includes photos, audio, and any text that you may put online. Treat others with **respect**, and don't stand by if you encounter any **cyberbullying**. If it becomes a problem, speak to a teacher or parent.

When you create online, make sure the sites you visit are trustworthy. A lock symbol in the address bar is a sign of safety. Consider how you found the site. Was it recommended by a teacher or did you find it randomly through an online search? If you question whether a site is trustworthy, exit it. Ask a trusted adult for help if you can't exit easily.

Checking the URL

Look at the website URL, or address. Addresses starting with https are more secure than those starting with http. You can also examine the type of **domain**. **Nonprofits** use ".org", e.g. www.commonsense.org. Government sites use ".gov", e.g. www.loc.gov. Educational sites often end in ".edu." The most common is ".com"—for businesses that usually make a profit from their sites. An example is www.amazon.com. They can sometime be less reliable than others.

Sharing Your Skills and Talents

Sharing digital creations expands our collective knowledge as a society. This means that the more ideas people share, the more that we can learn. It provides inspiration for other creative works. It can even bring about social change.

TheGoodCards.com is a game which challenges players to do good deeds. It started with two people who created an online gaming platform and mobile app. It encourages people to take action for social good—and shows how digital citizens contribute to the digital community in meaningful ways. What could you create that could inspire social change in your community?

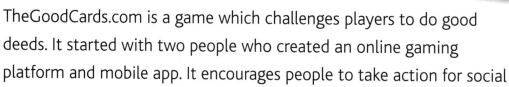

Natalie Hampton developed a simple app called Sit With Us. It connects teens looking for somewhere to sit at lunch with people who have room at their table. In middle school, Natalie always ate alone. She was bullied for it. She wanted to make sure no one sat alone again.

ts are short videos posted on Vimeo by fifth grader Olivia
Ledtje. She shares what she reading, thinking about, and
ing through social media. According to her website (http://
v.thelivbits.com), she is "excited that people get to see the
er of kids using the Internet in positive ways." Over 40,000
wers can be found on her "Mom-itered" Twitter account.

DIGITAL
YNAMO

technior
TECH + SENIOR

SHARON WANG, TECH TEACHER

In her teens, Sharon Wang started a
nonprofit organization called "Technior."
It stands for "technology" and "senior."
Sharon saw the power of technology
as a bridge between generations.
Young people adapt to new technology fast. They are **digital
natives**. They have never known anything but the digital world.
Most seniors were born decades before computers came into
existence. Technior puts tech-savvy teens together with seniors
who want to develop their online skills. Sharon's creative solution
to the challenges seniors face is digital citizenship in action!

Create a Smashing Good Show!

Using Buncee Education (or another school- or parent-approved digital tool), create a slideshow about your favorite hobby. It could be dancing or drawing, playing basketball or video games. Whatever it is, use the tips here and the information in this book to create a media mashup that will wow your friends!

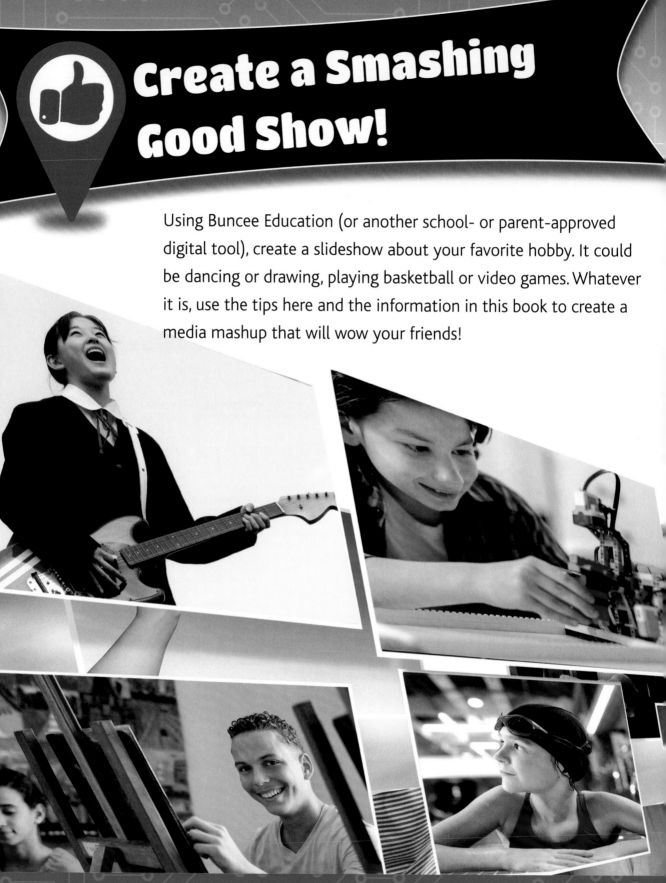

Follow these steps to get creating!

1. Decide on your slideshow topic.
2. Choose what types of media you would like to include in your slideshow. Are you going to add text? If so, write a draft, or first version, of your text now.
3. Will you add photos and/or artwork? Make image selections from Creative Commons, write up a list to see what can be found in the Buncee library, or make note of your own photos to be added. Be sure to add attribution statements for each image that is not your own. Add the attribution statements to a "Credits" page at the end of your storyline.
4. With a parent or teacher's assistance, sign up for a free Buncee account. You will need to have an email address.
5. Review the tutorials to get an understanding of how the site works.
6. Choose photos and/or artwork.
7. Add text.
8. Record new videos, or add existing videos, using AndroVid Video Editor from the App Store (or a similar program).
9. List "Credits" on final slide.
10. Review your work. Does it need tweaking? What do you need to do to make it better?
11. Rework until you are happy with the final product.
12. Share with your class, friends, or family.

Future Tech Check

Digital natives, like you, are connected with technology every day. In 2008, Apple opened its App Store. It had 5,000 apps by the end of its first year. Seven years later there were 1.75 million apps available. It is predicted that the store will hold over five million apps by 2020. Digital creation is booming. The digital future has no limit.

What will future digital creation include? It will see more people move from passive users to passionate inventors. You learn to code because you want to create, not just consume. You will expect more personalized and connected digital experiences.

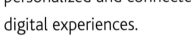

Artificial intelligence, augmented reality, and virtual reality will become even more integrated into every aspect of our lives. Alexa, Siri, Cortana, and other digital assistants will continue to develop and creatively weave themselves into the fabric of our digital world. Interactive digital storytelling will increase in popularity. Museums will continue to make educational visits even more digitally interactive. Schools will make leaps in promoting digital creativity and understanding of digital citizenship.

TECH TOOLBOX

The Gardens Between is a new puzzle game for PlayStation®4. In the game, two friends travel back and forth in time to uncover each garden's secret and share a story about friendship and growing up. It reveals an entire story without a single word. What ideas does it give you for your own digital storytelling creations?

Glossary

app A mobile program or application that is downloaded to a device

artificial intelligence The ability of computers or robots to think and behave like humans

attribution Identifying the source of a work

augmented reality A technology that puts a computer-generated image on top of someone's view of the real world

code Program instructions used on computers

copyright The exclusive legal right of a creator to print, publish, perform, or record material and to allow others to do the same

credit To publicly acknowledge someone in the creation of a work

critically To think critically is to ask questions, gather and analyze information, and make informed decisions

cyberbullying Bullying through electronic communication

digital Describing something characterized by electronic and computerized technology

digital community People who interact through the Internet or digital platforms

digital footprint The trail of data you create while using the Internet

digital natives A person brought up during the age of digital technology

distribute Give out

domain The name of a website

fair use Legal use of copyrighted material without the permission of the owner in a fair and reasonable manner that does not affect the value of the material or profits of the owner

infographic A visual image such as a chart or diagram that represents information or data

license Permission granted by the copyright holder to copy, distribute, display, change, or perform a copyrighted work

mashup New piece of work created by reusing and combining other digital creations

nonprofits Organizations that do not work for money—they often rely on donations and do work for social good

podcast A series of audio files that others listen to

productive Creating things and contributing to

profit Financial gain

respect To give something or someone the attention and/or admiration it deserves

search engine A program that searches for specific keywords on the World Wide Web

social media Websites and applications that let you create and share content with others

virtual reality A computer-generated simulation of an image or environment that can be interacted with a seemingly real way

Learning More

Websites

http://creativecommons.org
Learn about the Creative Commons organization and the six CC licenses; search for CC images, video, and audio you can use in your projects; and use the online tool to help you figure out which CC license is right for your work.

https://beinternetawesome.withgoogle.com/interland
You'll learn about online safety and citizenship as you play your way toward becoming Internet awesome!

https://www.commonsense.org/education/blog/15-best-tech-creation-tools
Visit the Common Sense Education website to explore the 15 best tech creation tools, and read other posts about amazing apps, games, websites, and tools that spark learning and creativity.

https://hatchcoding.com/center
View some student-created coding projects and see digital citizenship in action!

Books

Hatter, Clyde. *CoderDojo Nano: Building a Website.* Scholastic Inc., 2016.

Lauridsen, Craig. *iPad Animation: How to Make Stop Motion Movies on the iPad with iStopMotion, Garageband, and iMovie.* Acumen, 2014.

Takeuchi, Danny J. *Animation for Kids with Scratch Programming: Create Your Own Digital Art, Games, and Stories with Code.* Mentorscloud, 2015.

Wainewright, Max. *I'm a Scratch Coder.* Crabtree Publishing, 2018.

Index

About the Author

Megan Kopp is the author of more than 80 nonfiction books for children and hundreds of magazine articles. She flexes her online creativity with a blog and through social media. She loves apps that help her track steps on the trail or teach her a language.